lolo; /

14

D1554214

NEO-MELANESIAN-ENGLISH
CONCISE DICTIONARY

NEO-MELANESIAN-ENGLISH
CONCISE DICTIONARY

NEW GUINEA PIDGIN-ENGLISH

Compiled by
FRIEDRICH STEINBAUER

HIPPOCRENE BOOKS
New York

Library Resource Center
Renton Technical College
3000 N.E. 4th St.
Renton, WA 98056

499.5321 STEINBA 1998

Steinbauer, Friedrich.

Neo-Melanesian-Englis
concise dictionary

Copyright©1998 Hippocrene Books, Inc.

First published 1969 by Kristen Pres, New Guinea

For information, address:
HIPPOCRENE BOOKS, INC.
171 Madison Avenue
New York, NY 10016

ISBN 0-7818-0656-9

Printed in the United States of America

INTRODUCTION

This dictionary contains a list of about 1900 words of the New Guinea Pidgin language, which is also called Neo-Melanesian. The dictionary is a concise one, since it does not include all the words used by every segment of the population and in every dialect area. However, it does contain all the words, we hope, that are used universally in all areas of the Territory and by all speakers of the language. For this reason, it is particularly helpful to those first learning the language, since it gives the assurance to the learner that he will be understood wherever he goes. Technical words used only in special situations are not normally included.

Layout

Please note the following features of the way the dictionary is organized:

1) All words are listed alphabetically.
2) The meanings of the words with the same origin but having different meanings are separated by semi-colons (;) and written on separate lines. They are regarded, however, as being the same Pidgin word.
3) Homonyms, on the other hand, since they have a different origin, are listed separately.
4) The presentation of meanings for any word generally follows the following order: noun first, then adjective, verb, and adverb as required.
5) Transitive verbs are usually listed separately.
6) Words in brackets ( ) behind the listed word may normally be used interchangeably with the listed word.

Sources of Words

Preceding each listed word is an abbreviation of its language of origin. These abbreviations are listed below:

E – English
G – German
L – Latin
Sp – Spanish

On – Onomatopoetic
Mel – Melanesian
Mal – Malayan
Pol – Polynesian

Port – Portuguese	Gaz – from the Gazelle peninsula
Gr – Greek	in New Britain
E/G – from either	NI – New Ireland
English or German	? – Unknown

The percentage of the words in this dictionary from these sources are roughly as follows:

> from English – just over 80%
> from German – nearly 5%
> from Spanish, Portuguese, Latin, Greek
> and onomatopoetic words – nearly 5%
> from the Pacific area – nearly 7%
> Unknown – about 3%

Since it is likely that most of the unknown words come from Pacific languages, about 10% of the vocabulary probably comes from that area.

History of New Guinea Pidgin

No one knows exactly how New Guinea Pidgin began. It most probably grew out of the use of Beach-la-mar on the sugar plantations of Queensland during the last half of the last century. Beach-la-mar itself was a pidginized form of English found over wide areas of the Pacific. In all probability, most of the Latin, Greek, Spanish, Portuguese, Malayan, and Polynesian words found in New Guinea Pidgin came into it via Beach-la-mar.

Beach-la-mar was used primarily between Europeans and the natives of the Pacific Islands. But on the Queensland plantations, where New Guinea Pidgin developed from it, this aspect changed. The labourers themselves used it as the only possible method of communication among themselves, since they came from many different language groups. Some Melanesian words, especially those from the Gazelle Peninsula, were probably added to the vocabulary at that time. When these labourers returned to the Territory, the language proved useful to the German administration, and this is undoubtedly when many German words were added. Since the 1st World War, the use of Pidgin has spread over most of the Trust Territory and parts of Papua, mostly again through its use in intertribal communication. Most of the words added from this time on have again been from English.

6

Pronunciation

A few words of explanation about the pronunciation of Pidgin may be helpful to some readers. Generally speaking, it is essential to remember one rule. Just because a word comes historically from English or any other language, this does not mean that its pronunciation (or meaning) is the same as in the original language. When it becomes part of Pidgin, it takes on Pidgin pronunciation and meaning.

The orthography of Pidgin is generally phonetic. This means that each letter is pronounced in the same way whenever you find it. This is not true regarding the letter "p" and most of the vowels, but it is normally true in other instances. The following simple guide will be helpful.

a – pronounced as the *a* in father.

e – pronounced two ways, either as the *e* in ten, or as the *a* in day.

i – pronounced two ways, either as the *i* in hit, or as the *ee* in meet.

o – pronounced two ways, either as the *oa* in road, or as the *Au* in August.

u – pronounced two ways, either as the *oo* in fool, or as the *oo* in foot.

p – pronounced as the *p* in spill, not as the *p* in pill. (If you listen carefully, you will notice that there is much less breath emitted when saying the *p* of spill than there is for the *p* in pill.)

t – pronounced as the *t* in still, not as the *t* in till. (Same note applies as for *p* above.)

k – pronounced as the *k* in skill, not as the *k* in kill. (Same note applies as for *p* above.)

f – the sound is made by bringing both lips close together, rather than bringing the upper teeth into contact with the lower lip as in the English *f*.

v – the sound is again made with both lips, rather than the upper teeth and the lower lip as in the English *v*.

The remaining consonants are pronounced basically as in English. In some Pidgin dialects, there is much variation between the *l* and the *r*, no matter which is written. In standard Pidgin, the pronunciation follows what is written, although the *r* is shorter, with the tongue barely "flapping" back.

One final note. The pronunciation of the letter written *p* is pronounced as *f* in many cases, varying a bit from dialect to dialect. This will have to be learned by each speaker until the orthography is adjusted at this point.

The Usability of Pidgin

Those who do not know Pidgin well may assume that, because of its limited vocabulary, people are not able to use it to express themselves clearly in most areas of life. Fortunately, this is not true, as the wide acceptance of *Nupela Testamen* shows. Word combinations and varieties of word order in the sentence give a possible range of expression roughly equal to that of the vocabulary of the average European.

Pidgin is adequate in both vocabulary and concepts for whatever use the main body of Pidgin speakers wishes to make of it. There are some areas of Western culture which have not yet been used by the majority of Pidgin speakers, because those areas have not been assimilated into their own cultural patterns. For this reason, technical vocabulary in these fields is not widely known in Pidgin. When these cultural areas are assimilated into the way of life of the majority of the speakers of the language, the necessary vocabulary for expressing the concepts involved will be developed as it is in other languages – either by borrowing terms from another language or by creating new terms according to the word formation patterns already found in Pidgin itself.

Without a doubt, Pidgin is the most useful language in the Territory of Papua and New Guinea today. As you speak it, remember that it is a valid language by itself, not a garbled form of English. Only when you remember this will you be able to learn to speak it well. Then it will become very useful to you.

November 1969

NEO-MELANESIAN-ENGLISH
CONCISE DICTIONARY

A

Origin	Neo-Melanesian	English
On	a	exclamation of surprise; exclamation of interrogation
E	abris	to be apart from; alongside
E	abrisim	to fail, to pass by; to evade, detour
?	abus	pig, pork, meat; game, loot; delight
?	abusim	to garnish, to season; to mix, to mix up
E	adres	address
E	adresim	to address
L/E	Adven	Advent
L/E	Afrika	Africa; African
On	agai	what you say! exclamation
E	ai	eye; lid, tip, point
Mel	aiai	Malayan apple fruit and tree
?	aibika	plant with edible leaves
E	aidin, (yot)	iodine
E	aiglas	eyeglasses, spectacles
E	ailan	island
E	ain	iron, steel, metal; of iron, of metal; iron

E	ainim	to press with an iron
E	aipas	a blind person; blind
G/E	ais	ice
E	aiwara	tear
G/E	akis	axe, hatchet
G/E	alkohol	alcohol
L/G/E	alta	an altar
Mal	amamas	joy, gladness, delight; to rejoice, to be proud of; to flirt, to attract attention
?	amat	raw, uncooked
L/E	ambrela	umbrella
L/E	Amerika	America; American
E	ami	army
G	ananas, (painap)	pineapple
E	animal	animal
E	aninit	underneath, beneath, under
E	anian	onion, shallot
E	anis	ant
G/E	anka	anchor; to settle down, to stay
G/E	ankaim	to anchor something, to keep

11

Library Resource Center
Renton Technical College
3000 N.E. 4th St.
Renton, WA 98056

Origin	Neo-Melanesian	English
E	antap	the top, surface; on top, above, aloft; to be high, superior
E	apim	to raise, to lift up
E	apinun	evening, sunset
Gr/E	aposel	apostle
E	arakain	another kind; differently
E	arapela	another one, other
Mal	arere	border, limit, edge, side; alongside, next to; to wait for, to lie in ambush
E	arurut	arrowroot, starch
G/E	as	buttock, backside, anus; foundation, base, bottom, roots; origin, cause, reason, meaning
E	asasait	to take exercise, to drill
E	asde	yesterday
E	as ples	place of origin, home
E	as tok	mother language; meaning of saying
E	asembli	assembly
L/E	Asensen	ascension of Christ
E	aset	that's it exactly!
E	askim, (kwesten)	question; to ask, request, invite, inquire
G	asprin	Aspirin, Aspro
E	As Trinde	Ash Wednesday

12

Origin	Neo-Melanesian	English
?	asua	fault, blame
G	atebrin	atabrine
E	atensan	attention
E	ating	perhaps, suppose, probably (question indicator)
L/E	atun	Spanish mackerel, tuna fish
E	aua	hour
E	ausait	the exterior, appearance, outside
E	aut	to be gone, out, on the loose
E	autim	to divulge, to tell a secret
E	aven, (stov)	oven, stove

B

Origin	Neo-Melanesian	English
E	ba	bar
E	baga	a good-for-nothing person
E	bagarap	damaged, ruined, spoiled; badly hurt, injured; to be very tired, not well
E	bagarapim	to ruin something, wreck, hurt
E	bai	shall, will, intend
E	baibai, (gutbai)	bye-bye, goodbye
Gr/E	Baibel	Bible
E	baik, (baskol)	bicycle, bike

13

Origin (Ursprung)	Neo-Melanesian	English
E	baim	to buy, to purchase; to sell; to pay
G/E	bainat	bayonet, sword
Gaz	baira (hapap)	hoe
Gaz	bairaim (hapapim)	to hoe something
E	bak	pocket
G	bakbot	port side of a ship
E	baket	bucket, pail
E	baklain	rope, hawser
E	baksait	back, reverse side, rear; on the other side, behind; behind one's back
E	bakstua	bulkstore, warehouse
E/G	bal	ball
E	balaisim	to splice, to split
E/G	balas	ballast, load
Gaz	balus	dove, pigeon; aeroplane
On	bam	knock, hit, collision
E	bambai	after a while; shall, will, intend
On	bamim	to knock against, to smash
Sp	banana	banana
E	banara	bow (of bow and arrow)

14

Origin (Ursprung)	Neo-Melanesian	English
G	bang	bench
E	banis	bandage for sores; fence, wall, compound, enclosure; chest wall, ribs; brassiere
E	banisim	to bandage something; to fence in, surround
Gr	baptais (waswas)	baptism
Gr	baptaisim	to baptize, Christianize
Mal	baret	ditch, groove, corrugation, river
Mal	baretim	to drain by making ditches
L	barisom	pyrethrum plant
E	bas	bus
E	baset	budget
E	basket	basket
E	basketbal	basketball
E	baskol (baik)	bicycle
E	bastat	bastard, born "in the bush"
E	bata	butter
E	bataplai	butterfly
E	baten	button
E/G	bateri	battery
E	baut	curve, bend, turn; to turn, to curve
E	bebi	baby

Origin (Ursprung)	Neo-Melanesian	English
E	bek	bag, sack
E	bek	back
E	bekim	to give back, to pay back; to answer; to take revenge; to give repayment
E	bel	belly, stomach; womb, uterus; pregnant; heart, mind, emotions, thoughts; interior of something
E	belgut	present, gift, kindness
E	belhat	anger; angry, furious
E	bel isi	joy, relief, benevolence; enjoyed, content
E	bel pen	stomach ache
E	belo	signal, horn, bell; noontime
E	belo bek	early afternoon
E	beng	bank
E	beng	to collide, bang, smash
E	bengim	to collide with something, to smash something
E/G	bensin	benzine, petrol, gasoline
E/G	bet	bed; shelf, platform; nest
G	beten	prayer; to pray

16

Origin (Ursprung)	Neo-Melanesian	English
G/E	bia	beer
E	bihain	afterwards, later, in future; late
E	bihainim	to follow, imitate, obey
E	bihaintaim	late
E	bikbel	fat person; fat, stout
G	bikbel	water buffalo, carabao
E	bikbos	head manager
E	bikbrata	older brother
E	bikbus	deep jungle, the wilds
E	bikdaunbilo	hold of a ship
E	bikde	holiday, feast
E	bikdua	main entrance, main gate
E	bikgan	cannon
E	bikhet	a stubborn person; stubborn, disobedient, obstinate
E	bikhet man	a stubborn person
E	bikjas	chief judge
E	bikmasta	supreme master or ruler, head manager
E	bikmaunten	high mountain, peak
E	bikmaus	braggart, "big-mouth"; loudspeaker, amplifier; shouting, yelling; to shout, bark, yell; saucy, impudent

17

Origin (Ursprung)	Neo-Melanesian	English
E	bikmausim	to shout, yell at someone
E	bikmoning	very early, dawn
E	biknait	midnight, very late at night
E	biknem	generic name, common term; fame, reputation;
E	bikos	because
E	bikpela	big
E	bikples	main village; town; homeland, country; mainland (opposite to island)
E	bikpris	high priest, chief priest
E	bikrot	main road, highway
E	bikrum	living room, large hall
E	biksan	high noon, noonday sun
E	biksi	storm, stormy sea
E	biksolwara	ocean, open sea, deep sea
E	biktaun	big settlement, town, city
E	bikwin	wind, storm, hurricane
E	bilas	finery, adornment, decoration; showy clothes; mockery, ridicule; blasphemy; to put on finery, to dress
E	bilasim	to adorn, decorate, dress up
Port	bilinat	betelnut palm and its fruit

Origin (Ursprung)	Neo-Melanesian	English
E	bilip	belief, faith; to believe in
E	bilipim	to believe something
E	bilong	genitive marker: God's word; of (the possessive) house of mine; source, origin: fruit of a tree; showing purpose: water for drinking; denoting quality: a man who knows; therefore, for what reason? for this purpose; expression of attitude:
E	bilong wanem	why
?	bilum	netbag, bag, net covering; afterbirth, placenta
E	bin	bean
E/G	bin	auxilary to denote the perfective: been (with locative tendency)
Mel	binatang	bug, insect, small creeping things
G	binen	bee
E	Bipi	B.P., Burns Philp Company
E	bipo	before, formerly, previously
E	bipotaim	early, beforehand
Gaz	birua	enemy, opponent

Origin (Ursprung)	Neo-Melanesian	English
E	bis	beads, grass seeds
E	bisi	busy
E	bisipasin	diligence, eagerness
E	bisket	biscuit, cookie, cracker
E	bisnis	business, trade; clan, tribe, tribesman
E	bisnisman	business man
L/E	bisop	bishop
E	biugel	horn, trumpet, bugle
E	bladi	bloody (vulgar adjective)
E	blain	woven walls or matting
E	blak, blakpela	black, dark
E	blakbokis	flying fox
E	blakbot	blackboard
E	blakman	negro, coloured person; uncivilized person
E	blakskin	native, national, indigenous
E	blanket	blanket
E	blesim	to bless someone or something
E	blesing	blessing
E	blok	block, pulley; section, square of ca. 10 yards
G	blok	pad of paper
E	blokim	to block, obstruct; to raise or pull by pulley

Origin (Ursprung)	Neo-Melanesian	English
E	blu, blupela	blue
E	bluston	copper sulfate, antiseptic
G	blut	blood, pulse; sap
E	bodi	body
E/G	bo, bora	drill, bit
E	boi	boy, native labourer, servant; to work for as a helper
E	boil	boiling; to boil, to swirl
E	boilim	to boil something
E	boinim	to burn; to give a sound thrashing; to charm someone
E	bokis	box, trunk, case, carton; female genitals (euphemistic)
G	boksen	to box, fight with fists
E	bol	lead, solder; buckshot in cartridges; testicle, scrotum
E	bom	bomb
E	bomim	to bomb something
Mal	bombom	torch, flare
E	bop	bob, 1 shilling, 10 cents
G	borim	to drill
E	bos	boss, overseer, leader

Origin	Neo-Melanesian	English
E	bosim	to be in charge, rule over; to be owner of, to oversee
E	bosboi	work foreman, native overseer
E	boskru	boat's crew, sailors
E	boskuk	chief cook, chief steward
E	bot	boat, ship
E	botol	bottle, jar, vase
G	brait	width
E	brata	sibling of same sex: for boys a boy, for girls it is a girl
E	brata	brother, friend, fellow
E	bratasusa	siblings, brothers and sisters
E	brandi	brandy
E	bras	brush, steel brush or wool
E	bras	brass, copper
E	brasbel	small haversack, pouch
E	brasbel	brassiere
E/G	braun, braunpela	brown
E	brekpas	breakfast
E	bret	bread
E	brik	brick
E	bringim	to bring or take something or someone
E	bris	bridge, wharf

Origin (Ursprung)	Neo-Melanesian	English
E/G	bros	breast, chest
E	bros	brush
E	brosim	to brush something
E	brotkas	broadcast, transmission
G	bruder	religious brother
E	bruk	broken; to break, to burst
E	brukim	to break, tear, fold, bend, or split something; to cross over; dividing numbers
E	brum	broom, broomstick, duster
E	brumim	to clean, sweep; to collect, to steal; to defeat in battle
E	brumstik	broomstick, tough weed
?	brus	native leaf tobacco
?	buai	betelnut, fruit of Areca palm
E	buk	book, booklet
Gaz	buk	hill, hump, to be arched; swelling, boil, carbuncle, lump
Gaz	bukim	to toss, to buck
Mel	Buka	natives at Buka/Solomon Island;
	buka	very dark-skinned, coal black; crow
Gaz	bulit (laim)	sticky sap, resin, glue
Gaz	bulitim (laimim)	to glue something

E	bulmakau	cattle
E	bulsit	vulgar expression: shit
E	bun	bone, skeleton, framework; strength; essence of something
Gaz	bung	assembly, meeting, market; to gather, to assemble
Gaz	bungim	to gather something, crowd around
E	bus	bush, jungle, forest, wilds, woods; outpost, outstation
E	buskanaka	uncivilized man (abusive)
E	busnaip	bushknife, machete
E	busrot	path, small road in the woods
E	buswara	spring, creek in forest

D

E	dabol	double
E	dabolim	to double
E	dai (indai)	death; dead, unconscious
E	dai	to die, to faint, to be numb or paralyzed, or unconscious; to stop, to end, to cease; to long for, to desire
E	daiman	dead person, dying person, corpse

24

E	daimanples	limbo, place of departed souls
E	dais	dice
E	daisim (satu)	to dice
E	daiva	diver
E	daivim	to dive, to plunge, dip, submerge
Gaz	daka	betel pepper vine, root, leaf, chewed with betel nut itself
Gr/E	danamat	dynamite
E	das	dust
E	dasan	dozen
E	daun	down; deep, low; steep; low; humble, lowly; feeling lost, on the loosing side
E	daunbilo	below; long time ago
E	daunim	to overcome, overpower, defeat, suppress someone; to put down, swallow down; to humiliate someone
E	daunpasin	humility
E	de	day; time, season, weather
E/G	dek	deck
L/E	deliget	delegate
E	demim	to damn, condemn

Origin (Ursprung)	Neo-Melanesian	English
L/E	Desemba	December
E	desk	desk
E	dia	dear, precious; dear, expensive
Gaz/G	didiman	German agricultural officer, all agricultural workers
E	diksineri	dictionary
Gaz	dinau	debts, obligation
L/E	direkta	director, manager
E	dis	dish, basin, bowl
E	dispela	this, these
L/E	dispenseri	dispensary, clinic, aid-post
E	distrik	district
L/E	divosen	devotion
Gaz	diwai (tri)	wood, tree, log; wooden
Gaz	diwai kros	a cross
E	dok	dog
L/E	dokta	doctor, medical practitioner
E	dola	dollar, $
E	donki	donkey
E	doti	dirt, indecency; to be dirty
E	dotipela	dirty, indecent
E	drai	dry, dried up, hardened; healed

Origin	Neo-Melanesian	English
E	draidok	drydock, slipway for repairing
E	draipela	huge, strong, tremendous
E	draiv	drive, to drive
E	draiva	driver
E	draivim	to drive something
E	draiwara	low tide, ebb tide
E	dram	drum of iron, steel barrel
E	driman	dream; dreamer, sleepyhead, sleepwalker; to dream
E	dring	drink, beverage; to drink, to sip, to suck
E	dringim	to drink something
G/E	drip	green coconut, sprout
E	drip	to drift
E	dripman	pilgrim, wanderer
E	droim	to draw
E	drop	drop
E	du	instigation, provocation, temptation; to incite, tempt, woo
E	dua	door, gate, entrance
E	duim	to incite, force someone
E	duti	duty

E

Origin	Neo-Melanesian	English
E	edukesen	education department of the administration
Gr	eklesia (sios)	church
E	eksampel	example
L/E	eksekyutiv	executive
E	em	he, she, it; him, her, it
E	em	this, that
E	em tasol	that is all, it is over; that's it, that's right; here, right here
E	emti	empty
E	en	him, her, it (after the words "long" and "bilong" in unstressed position)
E	Englan	England, Britain
E	ensel	angel
On	ensa op	heave ho (when pulling)
E	ensin	engine, motor
E	ensinia	engineer, mechanic
Gr/E	Epifeni	Epiphany
L/E	Epril	April
G	esel	donkey
G	esik (viniga)	vinegar

28

E	et, etpela	eight, 8
E	etpos	aid post
Gr/E	evanselis	evangelist, preacher

F

E/G	fail	file; to rub, scrape, file
E/G	failim	to file something
E	faiv, faipela	five, 5
E	faktori	factory
E	famili	family
E	fauntenpen	fountain pen
L/E	Februeri	February
E	federesen	federation
L/E	Ferisi	Pharisee
E	fel	to fail
E	felim	to fail something
E	fifti	fifty, 50
E	fiftin	fifteen, 15
L/E	fiktri	fig tree
E	fit	feet in measuring
E	fiva	fever

Origin	Neo-Melanesian	English
E	flai	to fly (not the fly!)
E	foa, fopela	four, 4
E	fom	form, class
E	fom	bench
E	Fonde	Thursday
E	foti	forty, 40
E	fotin	fourteen, 14
E	Fraide	Friday
E	fran	front, bow of ship, driver's cabin; in the front
E	fri	free
E	ful	fool
E	fut	foot, leg
E	futbal	soccer, kickball

G

Origin	Neo-Melanesian	English
E/G	gaden	garden, planted field
Mel	galimbong	sheath containing coconut blossoms
Gaz	galip	Tahitian chestnut, any nut
Mel	gam	large cowrie shells

Origin (Ursprung)	Neo-Melanesian	English
E	gan (gewer)	gun
Gaz	garamut	wooden signal drum, slit gong
E	gat	to have, to own, to possess; there is, there are
E	gata	gutter
E	gavman	government, administration
E	gen	again, once more
E	gel	girl
G	gewer (gan)	rifle, weapon
E	gia	gear, gears
E	giaman	lie, nonsense; to lie, to deceive
E	giamanim	to trick, fool someone
?	giri	hill, small peak
?	girigiri	small cowrie shell used as decoration and currency
Sp	gita	guitar
E	givim	to give, offer, entrust; to punish with something
G/E	glas	glass; binoculars, field glasses; mirror; thermometer
G/E	glasim	to observe, to spy; to signal with a mirror; to take one's temperature, to examine medically; to learn by supernatural means

31

Origin (Ursprung)	Neo-Melanesian	English
G/E	glasman	a seer, one who sees future events, cult leaders
L/E	glori	glory
E	go	to go
E	goan	go ahead, go onward
E	goap	to go up, to climb
E	goapim	to climb upon; to copulate, to mate; to run over something
G/E	God	God
G/E	gol	gold
E	gol	goal
E	golip (kina)	goldlip shell, mother of pearl
G/E	gras	grass, lawn, fodder, hay; hair, fur, feathers
E	grasop	grasshopper
E	graun	ground, soil, earth, land, mud; property, land for lease
E	graunim	to hill up plants, put ground around
E	grevi (sos)	gravy, sauce
G	grifel (sletpensil)	slate pencil
?	grile	ringworm, tinea, skin desease; fish scales
E	grin, grinpela	green, fresh
E	gris	grease, fat; ointment

Origin (Ursprung)	Neo-Melanesian	English
E	gris	flattery, flirt; to flatter, to bribe
E	grisim	to grease, to oil, to lubricate; to flatter someone, talk someone into something
E	grisman	fat person; flatterer
E	gude	good day, hello!
Mel	guma	snail
G	gumi	rubber, plastic, eraser, elastic
Gaz	guria	trembling, tremor; earthquake; fear, fright; to tremble, shiver, be nervous, to be afraid; anxiously waiting for
E/G	gut, gutpela	good, attractive, fine
E	gut apinun	good evening! (not afternoon)
E	gutbai	good-bye, to take leave
E	Gut Fraide	Good Friday
E	gut moning	good morning!
E	gut nait	good night!
E	gutnem	good name, reputation
E	gutnius	gospel, good news
E	guttaim	time of peace; time of good weather

H

Origin	Neo-Melanesian	English
G	haiden	heathen, pagan; heathenish
G	haidenman	heathen, non-Christian
E	hailans	highland, interior of New Guinea
E	haisap	to hoist, raise
E	haisapim	to hoist, raise something
E	haisim	to hoist, raise something
E	haisin	hygiene, health education
E	hait	hidden, secret, concealed; to hide
E	haitim	to hide, protect something
E	haiwara (waratait)	high tide, flood
G	halo	Hello!
G/E	hama	hammer
G/E	hamaim	to hammer, to thrash
E	hamas	how much, how many
E	hambak	humbug, foolishness; boastfulness, vanity, pride; impudence, insolence; to be boastful, vain, insolent; to fool around, frolic noisily
E	hambakman	fool, braggart, loafer, playboy, cranky fellow, agitator

Origin (Ursprung)	Neo-Melanesian	English
G/E	han	hand, arm, foreleg of animals; handle; branch; symbol for religious impurity (i.e. menstruating women)
G/NI	han kais	left, left hand
G/E	han sut	right, right hand
E	handet	one hundred, 100
E	hangamap	to hang, to be dependent
E	hangamapim	to hang (up) something
E	hangre	hunger, famine, starvation; to be hungry
E	hani	honey; honey, sweetheart, love
E	hankap	handcuffs
E	hankisip	handkerchief
E	hanrait	handwriting, script; to write (longhand)
E	hanwas (was)	wristwatch
E	hap	a piece, remainder; partially; (giving direction) there
E	hap hap	half done, incompletely
E	hap hapim	to do half a job, cut in parts
?	hapap (baira)	hoe
?	hapapim (bairaim)	to hoe, to trim

Origin (Ursprung)	Neo-Melanesian	English
E	hapasde	the day before yesterday
E	hapim	to halve, divide in two; to fill partially full
E	hapkas	a half caste, a Eurasian; person adopted in other tribe; light-skinned natives
E	hapsait	side, opposite side
E	haptumora	the day after tomorrow
E	hariap	to hurry, hasten; quickly, fast, speedily
E	hariapim	to make someone hurry
E	harim	to hear, listen, heed; to perceive, understand; to notice, experience
E	hasis	hatch, or hold of a ship
E	hat	hat, cap, helmet
E	hat (hatwok)	difficult, hard
E	hat, hatpela	hot, warm; fiery, zealous, energetic
E	hatim	to heat, make something hot
E	hatwara	hot spring, hot water; sago pudding
E	hatwok (hat)	difficult, hard
G/E	haus	house, home, hut, dwelling
E	hauslain	village, hamlet
G	hebsen	pea

Origin (Ursprung)	Neo-Melanesian	English
E	hel	hell
Gr/E	helikopta	helicopter
E	helpim	helper, mediator
E	helpim	to help, replace, assist
E	hepi	happy
E	het	head, skull; top, peak, begining, spring
E	het kela	a bald-headed man
E	het klia	well instructed
E	het kliaim	to explain, instruct
E	hetman	headman, leader
E	hetpilo	neck support
E	hetwin	frontwind, headwind; to go head first, to dive
E	heven	heaven and sky, mostly heaven
E	hevi	load, problem, responsibility, blame; heavy, tired, sad; pregnant; difficult
G/E	hia	here
E	hinsis (penda)	hinges
E	hip	heap, pile
E	hipim	to heap, pile something
E	hivap	to heave up, raise, hoist
E	hivapim	to raise, hoist something
G	hobel (plen)	plane of carpenters

Origin (Ursprung)	Neo-Melanesian	English
G	hobelim (plenim)	to plane, make smooth
E	holan	hold on, wait!
E	holi	holy, sacred
E	Holi Spirit	Holy Spirit
E	holide	holiday
E	holim	handle; to hold, hold on to
E	holim	to keep, be faithful, observe
E	holiman	saint, holy person
E	holipela de	church feast, a holy day.
E	hotel	hotel, pub
E	hos	horse
E	huk	hook, barb
E	hukim	to hook, catch something; to entice, allure someone
E	hul	hole, pit, cave, grave
E	husat	who, (not a relative pronoun)

I

E/?	i	untranslatable predicate marker: separately written between subject and predicate, but not after first and second person singular and first person plural inclusive; also between nouns as subject and predicate; also with auxiliary verbs according to the above mentioned rule
E	ia	ear, hearing
E	iapas	hard of hearing, deaf; stupid
E	iapen	earache
L/E	ileksen	election
L/E	ilektim	to elect
E	inap	enough, sufficient, fit; right size, ripe; to be suited for, to be able; till, until, up to, about
E	inapim	to satisfy, give enough
E	indai (dai)	death; dead
L/E	independens	independence
E	Inglis	English
E	ing	ink
E	ingpen	pen
E	ins	inch, measuring unit

Origin (Ursprung)	Neo-Melanesian	English
E	insait	the interior, the inside; meaning, content of something; to participate, be with; inside of, within, in, into
L/E	integresen	integration, fusion
L/E	interes	interest on money
E	is	east
E	isi	softly, gently, quietly, easily
E	isi isi (slo)	carefully, slowly
E	isipasin	gentleness, mildness, calmness
E	isipela	soft, gentle, quiet, easy
E	Ista	Easter
E	ivening	evening, late evening

J

Origin (Ursprung)	Neo-Melanesian	English
E	jak	jug, pitcher
L/E	Janyueri	January
E	Japan	Japan, Japanese people
E	jas	judge
E	jasim	to judge, hold court, decide, pass sentence
E	jek	jack

E	jekim	to jack up, elevate something
E	jem	jam, marmalade
E	jem	germ
E	Jeman	German
E	Jemani	Germany
E	Jemantaim	days of German rule before World War I
E/L	Jerusalem	Jerusalem
E	jip	jeep, car
E/L	Jisas	Jesus
E	join	to join, associate, unite
E	joinim	to join together
E/L	Juda	Jew
E/L	Julai	July
E/L	Jun	June

K

E	ka	car, wagon, automobile
E	kabis	cabbage
E	kago	cargo, supplies; household-ware, belongings; expected goods from the world of the ancestors

41

Origin (Ursprung)	Neo-Melanesian	English
E	kagoboi	labourer, carrier
Pol	kaikai	food, meal; to eat, chew, feed on
Pol	kaikaim	to eat something, bite something, chew something
G	kail	wedge
G	kailim	to put a wedge between
E	kain	kind, sort of
E	kain kain	all kinds of, various
NI	kais (lep)	left, the left side
NI	kaisim	to aim to the left
G	kaisa	emperor
G	kakalak (kokoros)	cockroach; parasitic insects; disliked persons
?	kakang (nilwaia)	barbed wire
?/On	kakaruk	hen, chicken; rooster, fowl
Mal	kakatu	cockatoo; pincers; vulva
G	kakau (koko)	cocoa tree and fruit
E	kaki	khaki colour, yellow-brown
Mel	kal	a certain bird in New Guinea
E	kala	colour
E	kalabus	calaboose (Amer.) gaol, jail; cage, box; safety pin; imprisioned, trapped, cornered

Origin (Ursprung)	Neo-Melanesian	English
E	kalabusim	to imprison, arrest, lock up; to hold up, stop, delay
E	kalabusman	prisoner, captive
?	kalang	feathers of a bird's tail; earring
E	kalap	jump, leap; to jump, spring, leap; to be astonished, amazed; to mate
E	kalapim	to jump over
?	kalapa	exclamation of sympathy; to mourn with, sympathize
G/E	kalenda	calendar
E/On	kalkalap	to dance, jump up and down
?	kaluk	native pillow, head rest
E	kam	to come
E	kaman	come on
E	kamap	to come up, appear, arise, grow; to begin, start; to come to, arrive, reach
E	kamapim	to begin, to originate, institute, invent; to reveal, bring to light
E	kamaut	to come out
E	kamautim	to pull out, harvest; to confess, reveal
Mal	kambang	lime, chewed with betelnut; the gourd filled with lime; gourd used as genital covering

43

E	kamda	carpenter, joiner, woodworker
E	kamdaman	carpenter, joiner, cabinetmaker
E	kam daun	come down! to come down
G/E	kamel	camel
E	kampani	company, squadron; company, business concern; term for private enterprise
E	kampani masta	businessman, trader
?	kan	vulva, female genitals
Pol	kanaka	"man", uncivilized native (remote people, abusive term); native villager
Mal	kanda	cane, rattan, stick
Mal	kandaim	to thrash, cane someone
E	kandel	candle
E	kandelstik	candlestick
E	kandere	all relatives from the mother's side: uncle, nephew, niece, cousin, (especially mother's brother)
E/L	kandidet	candidate
Gaz	kangal	plumage, plumes, crest feathers; head adornment for dancing
E	kantri	country
E/Sp	kanu	canoe, outrigger boat
E	kap	cup
E	kapa	tin, galvanized roofing iron; fingernail, hoof, toenail

E	kaparesa	razor blade
E	kapet	carpet, mat, rug
Gaz	kapiak	breadfruit tree and its fruit
Mal	kapok	kapok tree, cotton
E	kapot (sarang)	cupboard, sideboard
E	kapsait	to capsize, overturn, upset; to overflow, spill over
E	kapsaitim	to pour out, spill something; to turn over something
NI	kapul	opposum, tree kangaroo, cuscus
E	karamap	package, parcel, packet; to be covered up
E	karamapim	to wrap, cover something; to hide, conceal something
?	karanas	crushed coral, coral gravel
E	karapela (propela)	propeller
E/Mal	kari	curry, Indian spice
E	karim	to carry, bring, take; to suffer, endure, bear; to bring forth, give birth
E	karim lek	petting game with crossed legs on partners' thighs
E	karis	carriage, wagon
E	karkarim	to carry around continuously
?	karuka	pandanus or screw pine; mat, raincoat; trough, container of pandanus tree splittings
G/E	kas	cask, barrel, drum

45

Origin (Ursprung)	Neo-Melanesian	English
?	kas	pride, trump, effect, boast
Mal	kasang (pinat)	peanut
?	kaskas	scabies, a skin disease
E	kastam	duty, custom, customs office
E	kastat	custard
E	kaswel	castor oil
E	kat	card, playing cards
E	kat	cut
E	katim	to cut, fell something; to interrupt, delete
E	katapila	caterpillar tractor; caterpillar
Gr/E	Katolik (Popi)	Catholic;
E	katres	cartridge, shell
Gaz	kaukau	sweet potato
E	kaun	to count
E	kaunim	to count something; to read
E	kaunsil	council, member of the council
?	kavang	betel palm flower sheath
?	kavivi	hawk
?	kawiwi	betelnut (secondary variety)
E	kebin	cabin
E	kek	cake

Origin (Ursprung)	Neo-Melanesian	English
E	kela	clear, bald, bare
E	kem	camp
E	ken	a can, jug
E	ken	to be willing, may
E	kep	cap; detonator, fuse
E	kepten	captain
E	kerasin	kerosene
E	kerot	carrot
E	kes	case, box, carton
E	keteka	caretaker
E	ki	key; faucet
Gaz	kiap	government official
Gaz	kiau	egg; pill; light globe
Gaz	kibung (bung)	meeting; to gather, hold a meeting
E	kik	kick, play soccer
E	kikbal	soccer ball, game of soccer
E	kikim	to kick someone or something, to repulse
G/E	kil	keel, ridge, spur of mountain
E	kilim	to beat, strike, thrash; to knock someone out; to hurt, make sick

Origin (Ursprung)	Neo-Melanesian	English
Gaz	kina (golip)	goldlip shell, oyster, mussel
?	kindam	lobster, crayfish, crab; prawn
E	king	king, ruler
E	kingdom	kingdom
E	kinin	quinine, anti-malarial drug
E	kirap	rising; to get up, awake, start; getting excited
E	kirap nogut	to be surprised, shocked, angry, to wonder
E	kirapim	to awaken someone, raise; to start, begin something
E	kis	kiss; to kiss
E	kisim	to take, get; to obtain, receive
E	kiwi	shoe polish (brand name)
Mal	klambu (taunam)	mosquito net
E	klap	club, club room
E	klas	class, grade
E	klaut	cloud, sky, firmament
E	klautbruk	cloudburst, thunderstorm
E	kleva	clever
E	klia	clear, pure, open; intelligible; get out of the way

Origin (Ursprung)	Neo-Melanesian	English
E	kliaim	to clear off, remove something; to clear up, explain something
E	klin, klinpela	clean, healed
E	klinim	to clean
E	klinik	clinic, hospital
E	klinpasin	purity, chastity
E	klok	clock, watch, hour; heart
E	klos	dress, clothes (of materials)
E	klosap	nearly, almost
E	klostu	close to, near, nearby; nearly
E	kok	penis; lid, small tap, petcock, cork
?	koki	large white cockatoo bird
E	koko (kakau)	cocoa
?	kokomo	hornbill, bird with large beak
G/E	kokonas	coconut palm and its fruit
E	kokoros (kakalak)	cockroach
E	kol, kolpela	cool, cold, fresh; pleasant
E	kolim	to cool something; to make cool, pacify someone
E	kolim	to call, tell, recite
L/G	kolekta	collection, offering
E	kolsiot	pullover, sweater

Origin (Ursprung)	Neo-Melanesian	English
E	kolta	coal tar, tar, pitch, creosote
E	kolwin	off-shore wind, breeze
E	kom	comb; horn or comb of animals
E	komim	to comb
E	komiti	committee, section; member of a council
?	komokomo	cowrie shell (medium size)
G/E	kompas	compass
L/E	komunion	Holy Communion
E	kon (mais)	corn, maize
E	kona	corner
E	konaston	corner stone, border stone, boundary stone
?	konda	paper money
L/E	konfemesen	confirmation
E	Kongkong	Chinaman, Malayan
L/E	kongrigesen	congregation
E/F	koniak	cognac
E	konprens	conference, meeting
E	kontrak	contract, agreement
E	kopi	coffee
E	kopibuk	copybook, exercise book
E	kopra	copra, dried coconuts
G	kopstik	bridle, rein

Origin (Ursprung)	Neo-Melanesian	English
E	kopul	corporal, military leader
E	kos	course, instruction class; course, compass
E	kostim	to cost, amount
E	kot	court, lawsuit, trial, accusation, judgment
E	kotim	to bring one to court
On	kotkot	small crow, raven
E	kotren	raincoat
E	krai	cry, weeping, mourning; sound, call, noise; to cry, call, weep, mourn; make noise, squeak; to long for, desire, think of one who is absent
G	kraide (sok)	chalk
L/E	Kraist	Christ
E	kramsel	conch chell, clam shell
E	kranki	wrong, incorrect; stupid, clumsy, awkward
E	kraun	crown
E	Krismas	Christmas;
E	krismas	celebration, feast, dancing year, age
E/G	Kristen	Christian

Origin (Ursprung)	Neo-Melanesian	English
E	kroba	crowbar
E	kros	anger, ill-humor; to quarrel, be angry
E	krosim	to scold someone; to be angry with someone
?	kru	sprout, bud, young shoot, seedling
E	krungut	cooked, twisted, bent, warped
E	krungutim	to bend, twist something; to press down, crush, step on; to distort, ruin
E	krungutman	trouble-maker, crooked man
E	kuk	cook; wife; to cook to be defeated, to lose
Gaz	kuka	crab
E	kukamba	cucumber
E	kukboi	kitchen helper, cook
E	kuki (bisket)	cooky, biscuit
E	kukim	to cook, bake, roast something; to burn, heat something; to defeat, destroy
Gaz	kukurai	chief of a tribe
Gaz	kulau	young, green coconut; any undeveloped boy or girl
?	kumu	kind of spinach, water cress, vegetable

Origin (Ursprung)	Neo-Melanesian	English
?	kumul	bird of paradise
Mel	kumurere	eucalyptus tree
Gaz	kunai	grass, alang-alang grass, grassland
Mel	kundu	drum, hand drum, tom-tom
Mel	kurita	octopus
?	kurakum	big red ant
E	kus	cough, cold, mucus; to cough, sneeze
NI	kusai	to deceive jokingly
NI	kuskus (seketeri)	clerk, secretary, procurator
E	kwaia	choir, chorus
E	kwesten (askim)	question
E	kwik	fast, quickly
E	kwiktaim	soon, in a short time, right away
NI	kwila	ironwood, ironwood tree
E	kwin	queen

L

Origin	Neo-Melanesian	English
E	laik	wish, desire; will; love; to like to, want to, wish to; to be ready, to be about to
E	laikim	to like, want, desire something
G	laim (bulit)	glue
G	laimim (bulitim)	to glue something
E	lain	line, row; rope, cord; clan, ancestral line; age group, grade, group; standing in line; to learn, study
E	lainim	to line up someone, something; to put in order, arrange, make ready; to learn, study; to teach someone something
E	laip	life (especially spiritual life)
E	laisens	license
E	lait	light, flash, flame; light, bright, burning; to light, shine, to be shiny
E	laitim	to light something, set fire to
E	laitning	lightning, fireworks

Gaz	laka	will you? won't you? don't you?
		  isn't that right? (at the end of a
		  question only)

Origin (Ursprung)	Neo-Melanesian	English
E	laki	luck, lucky as name of card game; something extra fine; to gamble, play a card game
E	lam	lamp
E	Landrova	Landrover
Mel	lang	fly
E	lap	laughter; to laugh, smile, laugh at
E	lapim	to laugh at
Pol	laplap	loincloth, waistcloth, material
?	lapun	old, aged person; old, elderly, aged; experienced
E	larim	to let, leave, allow
E	las	last, at the end
E	lasde	end of the world, the last day
E	lata	ladder, steps, staircase
Mal	laulau	Malay apple tree, apple
?	laup	New Guinea walnut tree
G	laus	louse, flea
E	lego	to let go, let down, release
E	legoim	to drop, let something down
E	lek	leg, foot; footprint, trace, mark
E	lektrik	electricity, power; electrician; electric

Origin (Ursprung)	Neo-Melanesian	English
E	lemanet	lemonade, lolly water
E	Len	Lent, time of passion
E	lep (kais)	left
E	lepa	leprosy, Hansen's disease
E	lepaman	leper, leprosy patient
G	lepra	leprosy, Hansen's disease
E	les	to be lazy; to be tired, exhausted
E	lesbaga	lazy fellow, a good for nothing
E/L	lesislativ	legislative
E	leson	lesson
E	let	belt, leather belt, leather
E	let	late
E	leta	letter of alphabet, letter
E	letes	lettuce
E	level	a carpenter's level even, level, straight, smooth
E	levelim	to level, make something smooth
G	lewa	liver, heart, seat of affections; desire, something one craves; darling, sweetheart, honey
E	lik	leak, hole; to leak
Gaz	liklik	little, small; a bit, somewhat, a little

Origin (Ursprung)	Neo-Melanesian	English
NI	limbum	Areca palm (leaves used for mats and baskets, trunk used for flooring)
Gaz	limlimbur	a walk, stroll, an outing; to take a walk, stroll leisurely, move slowly
E	lin	lint, gauze used in dressings
E	lindaun	to bend down, lean forward
E	lip	leaf
E	lip	leave, holiday, vacation
E/G	lista	list, register
E	litimap	to lift up, to be lifted up
E	litimapim	to lift something, pick up something; to praise someone
Gr/E	litugi	liturgy
E	lo	law, custom, rule
E	lok	lock
E	lokap	to be locked up
E	lokapim	to lock up something
E	lokim	to lock something
E	loli	candy, lollies
E	loliwara	lemonade, fruit juice, carbonated beverage
E	loman	lawyer, solicitor
Mal	lombo	red pepper, chillies

Origin (Ursprung)	Neo-Melanesian	English
E	long	used for nearly all prepositions: in, at, on, with, under, from, by;
		used with indirect objects: i.e. give the book to me;
		in adverbial phrases: amidst, near, i.e. "on top of" the house; used as comparative particle: than
E	long	length
Gaz	longlong	stupidity, foolishness, ignorance; to be stupid, ignorant; to be confused, stunned; to be drunk, not accountable;
		crazy, insane
E	longpela	long, tall, high
E	longtaim	a long time,
E	long wanem	what for
E	longwe	distant, far away, long way off
E	lori	lorry, truck
Pol	lotu	religious service, worship; to worship;
		a particular denomination
Pol	lotuim	to worship someone
E	luk (lukluk)	looks, appearance;
E	lukaut	to look out, watch out for, beware of, look for, watch for; to look after, care for; woe unto you!

Origin (Ursprung)	Neo-Melanesian	English
E	lukautim	to take care of, look after, watch over, provide for; to look for, search for
E	lukim	to see something; to shine on, look at; to visit
E	lukluk (luk)	looks, appearance; to look, watch, glance
E	luklukim	to watch something
E/Sp	luksave	to recognize; to find out
E	luksi	to examine, test, check
Gaz	luluai	tribal chief appointed by the government
E	lum	loom for weaving
E	lumim	to weave
E	lus	to be lost, to be gone; to be loose, untied, sprained; to be past,
E	lusim	to lose, spend something; to lose, forfeit; to leave, leave behind, desert, abandon, miss; to forget; to loosen, untie; set free
E/G	Luteran	Lutheran

M

Origin	Neo-Melanesian	English
E	mail	mail
E	mail	a mile
E	mais (kon)	corn, maize
G	mak	monetary unit, German Mark, shilling
E	mak	mark, sign, design, scar, tattoo, footprint; characteristic; goal post for soccer
E	makim	to mark, sketch something; to appoint, assign, select, nominate; to promise; to aim, point at; to imitate, mimic, copy
E	makmak	pattern designs of colour; of various colours, with design
Gaz	mal	bark loin covering, G-string, bush clothing for men
Mal	Malai	a Malay, an Indonesian
?	malambur	herring, special fish
E/G	malaria	malaria, feverish disease
?	maleo	eel
Gaz	malolo	rest, recess, free time; to rest, relax
Mel	malumalum	soft, swampy, spongy; tender

Origin (Ursprung)	Neo-Melanesian	English
E	mama	mother, grandmother, aunt; female owner of a thing; nut of bolts and screws
E	mamapapa (papamama)	parents
Mal	mambu	bamboo; bamboo flute, ritual flute; bamboo as a cooking pot; pipe, tube
?	mami	type of yam
E	man	man, husband; human being, person; male
E	manabus	bushman, uncivilized man, savage
E	Mande	Monday
L	mandor	overseer, spokesman, leader
Mel	mangal	strong desire; to desire strongly, long for; envy, covet, yearn for
Mel	mangalim	to covet something
?	mangas	a certain tree of which the leaves are used for smoking
E	mango	mango tree and its fruit
E	mangro	mangrove tree; mangrove swamp
E	mani	money
E	maniok (tapiok)	manioc, edible tuber, cassava

Origin (Ursprung)	Neo-Melanesian	English
E	manki	monkey; boy, uninitiated boy, schoolboy; male servant, houseboy
E	mankimasta	personal servant, valet
E	manmeri	people, men and women
E	manua	man-o-war, battleship
E	marasin	medicine, drugs; means, admixture; beverage, liquor
Gaz	marila	love-spell, love-charm; magic for gardens and animals to raise fertility
Gaz	marilaim	to charm, bewitch, put a spell on
Gaz	marimari	pity, mercy, grace, patience; to have mercy, to pity
E	marit	marriage; to be or get married
E	maritim	to marry someone
E	marmar	a rain tree
E/L	Mas	March
E/G	mas	mast, flagpole, long post
E	mas	must, should, has to, have to
E	mas	to march
Gaz	masalai	nature spirits, thought to be in forests, rivers, rocks, winds; bugbear

62

(Ursprung) Origin	Neo-Melanesian	English
E	masin	machine, engine
E	masis	match, matches
E	masket	musket, gun, rifle, cannon
G?	maski	it does not matter, who cares; despite, in spite of; forget about it, leave it
E	masta	master, ruler, lord; in general a European
E	masta mak	surveyor
E	mastet	mustard
E/G	mat	mat
?	matakiau (wanai)	blind in one eye
?	matmat	cemetery, burial place, grave
Gaz	mau	ripe; rotten
E	maunten	mountain, hill, ridge, heap
E	Maunten Oliv	Mount of Olives
E	maus	mouth, snout, lip; opening; entrance; voice, talk
E	mausgras	beard; bearded
E	mauspas	a mute, dumb, tongue-tied person; to be mute, dumb, tongue-tied
E	mausogan	mouth organ, harmonica

63

Origin (Ursprung)	Neo-Melanesian	English
E	mauspen	to be tired, have pain in the mouth
E	Me	May
E	medal	medal
E	mekanik	mechanic, engineer
E	mekim	to make, create; to cause; to force; to do, act, behave
E	meknais	to shiver, shake, rattle
E	meknois	to make noise
E	mekpas	bundle, roll, parcel
?	melek (wara)	semen
E	melon	watermelon
E	memba	member
On/NI	meme	goat
E	meri	woman, wife, girl; female, feminine
G	meta (rula)	ruler, yardstick, measure, meter
G	metaim	to measure something
E	mi	I, me
E	miks	mixed
E	miksim	to mix something
E	mining	meaning

Origin (Ursprung)	Neo-Melanesian	English
E	minit	minute
E	minits	minutes, notes
E	mipela	we (excluding the person spoken to)
E/L	mirakel	miracle
E/L	misin	mission as a task; a mission as a body; missionary, preacher
E	misinari	missionary
E	misis	Mrs., any European woman; nowadays also used to address any married woman; queen in a card suit
?	mismis	clan brother; mating of fowls and birds
E	mit	meat, flesh
E	miting	meeting
E	mitupela	we two, both of us (excluding the person spoken to)
E	moa	more, further; denotes comparative degree used before adjectives and adverbs; denotes: very, after adjectives and adverbs
E	mobeta	better
?	mon	New Guinea walnut tree; high-prowed canoe without outrigger in East Melanesia

65

Origin (Ursprung)	Neo-Melanesian	English
E	moning	morning
E	moningtaim	in the morning, early
?	moran	python snake
?	morota	pandanus palm edible red, greasy fruit of that palm (also called: marita); sago palm leaf roofing
E	mosen	parliamentary motion
Sp	moskito	mosquito
?	mosong	felt, fine hairs, fuzz, the nap on cloth; to be fuzzy, hairy
E	motoka	motorcar, car, auto, truck
Gaz	muli	lemon, all citrus fruits
?	mumu	earth-oven-steam-cooking; meal prepared in such a pressure cooking pit
?	mumuim	to pressure cook something
?	mumut	bush rat, bandicoot, marmot; hoarder, profiteer; to hoard, gather up; to scavenge, to remove sanitary bucket
?	mumutim	to scavenge something, collect castoffs and hoard them
E	mun	moon; month; menstrual period

Origin (Ursprung)	Neo-Melanesian	English
Gaz	muruk	cassowary, kind of ostrich
E/G	musik	music
?	musmus	bedbug
E	muv	to make a parliamentary motion
E	muvi	the movies, pictures

N

?	na	and, and then; so, and so, therefore
?	na wanem	of course!
E	nabaut	about, around, in various directions, roundabout; aimlessly, carelessly, here and there
E	nain, nainpela	nine, 9
E	nainti	ninety, 90
E	naintin	nineteen, 19
E	naip	knife
E	naip skru (poketnaip)	pocket knife
E	nais, naispela	nice, beautiful, pretty, wonderful
?	nais	to shiver, shake
?	naisim	to shake something
E	nait	night, actually about 7-11 p.m.

Origin (Ursprung)	Neo-Melanesian	English
E	namba	number, a numeral; mark of rank or office, sign of authority; sign of classification
E	namba tu	second, the second one
E	namba wan	first, the first one
E	nambaim	to number, count something
E	nambatu	second best, of minor importance
E	nambawan	first class, best, most important
E	nambis	beach, shore, coast, seaside
E	namel	middle, centre; amidst, in the middle, between
E	namelman	mediator, arbiter, referee
E	napkin	napkin, serviette
E	narakain	different, differently, odd
E	narapela	another
E	nating	nothing, in vain, useless; empty; just, only, simply, merely; for no reason; bare, naked
?	natnat	mosquito, gnat
E	nau	now, the present time
E	nek	neck, throat; voice, melody, tune
E	neks	next

Origin (Ursprung)	Neo-Melanesian	English
E	nektai	necktie
E	nem	name; reputation
E	nes	nurse
E	netif	a native
?	ngong	deaf-mute, ignorant
E	nil	needle; shot, injection
E	nil	nail, thorn
E	nildaun	to kneel down
E	nilim	to nail something
E	nilwaia (kakang)	barbed wire
E	nius	news
E	niuspepa	newspaper
E	no	not
E	no (o)	or
E	no gat	not to have, not to be
E	nogat	no, nothing; yes (to a negative question); no (to a positive question)
E	nogut	no good, bad, evil, wicked; wrongly, badly, incorrectly; lest, else, otherwise; very, excessively

Origin (Ursprung)	Neo-Melanesian	English
E	nogutim	to spoil, damage, harm something
E	nois	noise
E	noisim	to make noise
E	no ken	not to be willing, don't have to, not to be allowed to; by no means!
E	noken	horizontal timber in house, midrib of sago or coconut palm leaves
E	not	north
E	Novemba	November
E	Nu Ailan	New Ireland
E	Nu Briten	New Britain
E	Nu Gini	New Guinea
E	nupela	new, fresh; recently
E/Gr	Nupela Testamen	New Testament
E	nus	nose, top; prow, ridge of house
E	Nuyia	New Year's Day

O

Origin	Neo-Melanesian	English
On	o	oh! at the end of a word if somebody calls, (without meaning);
E	o (no)	or
E	oda	order
E	oda	a command
E	odaim	to order something
E/L	odinesen	ordination
E	ofa	offering, sacrifice
E	ofaim	to offer something
E	ofis	office, official room
E	ofisa	officer
E/L	Ogas	August
E	oksen	auction; available; for sale, as a prostitute
E/L	Oktoba	October
E	ol	they, them; before nouns as sign of plural
E	olaboi (olaman)	exclamation: Goodness me! My word! Good heavens! Think of it!
E	olde	every day, daily
E	olgeta	all, every; altogether, completely, wholly
E	olpela	old, worn out

Origin (Ursprung)	Neo-Melanesian	English
E	Olpela Testamen	Old Testament
E	olsem	thus, in this way; similar to, like, such, as if
E	olsem na	and so, therefore, accordingly
E	olsem wanem	how? how can it happen?
E	oltaim	all the time, always
E	oltaim oltaim	forever, never ceasing, eternally
E	op	open, unlocked
E	opim	to open, unlock something
E	optin	tin opener
E	orait	O.K., all right, very well; good for, suitable, salutary; to agree to; conjunction: so, well, then
E	oraitim	to fix, straighten, cure, heal something
E	Ostrelya	Australia, Australian
E	ots	oats
E	ova	to turn over
E	ovaim	to turn something over

P

Origin	Neo-Melanesian	English
E	paia	fire; to be on fire, burn, catch fire; to scold, get angry
E	paiaman	fireboy (for copra drier); fireman
E	paiawut	firewood
E	pailot	pilot
E	painap (ananas)	pineapple
E	painim	to find, discover something; to be subject to a problem; to look for, seek
E	paintri	pine tree
E	paip	pipe for smoking; water pipe or drain pipe
E	pairap	crash, noise, sound, percussion; to explode, go off, crackle; to chatter, be noisy; to be furious
E	pairapim	to blow up, fire off something
E/Gaz	pait	fight, war, quarrel; to fight
E/Gaz	pait	something of sharp, sour taste
E	paitim	to hit, strike, beat, hurt, knock; to make one sick, senseless to sting, bite, make drunk
G/E	paket	pocket
E	Palamen	Parliament
NI	palai	lizard, gecko, iguana, monitor

Origin (Ursprung)	Neo-Melanesian	English
Mel	palpal	the coral tree, used to make growing fences
E	Pam Sande	Palm Sunday
E	pam	pump, air pump, tyre pump
E	pam	heart, pulse
E	pamim	to pump, inflate
E	pamkin	pumpkin
?	pamuk	unchastity, prostitution; to fornicate
NI	pangal	sago palm leaf stalk and stem; thin, skinny, meagre
E	pankek	pancake
L	papa	father, uncle, guardian; male owner, caretaker of something
L	Papa Santu (pop)	Pope, Holy Father
?	papai	mushroom
South Am.	papaia	fruit of the pawpaw tree
?	papait	sorcery, love spell
L	papamama (mamapapa)	parents
Gr/E	paradais	paradise
Gr/E	paragraf	paragraph
E	pas	letter, pass, note, permission

Origin (Ursprung)	Neo-Melanesian	English
E	pas	ahead; fast, firm, firmly; to be dense, crowded, tight; to be firmly held, to be stuck; to be blocked, closed shut
E	pasim	to fasten, tie something; to close, shut, wall in; to hold back someone
E	pasin	fashion, custom, manner, conduct, way of life, behaviour
E	pasindia	passenger
E	pasis	passage, bay, throughroad; place of rest, haven, harbour
E	paslain	in front, first in line
E	pasman	leader, one who goes before
E	Pasova	Passover
E	paspas	armlet, bracelet, armband
E	pastaim	first, at first
L/E	pasto	pastor, Reverend
E	pat, patpela	fat, stout
L	Pater	Father, priest
E	pati	party, social meeting; party, political group
Sp	pato	duck, drake
E	patrol	patrol; to go on a patrol

75

Origin (Ursprung)	Neo-Melanesian	English
E	paul	fowl, chicken
E	paul	to be fouled up, mixed up, twisted
E	paulim	to foul up, mix up, twist
E	paun	Australian pound in money, £
E	paura	gunpowder, any explosive; talcum powder
E	paus	pouch, suitcase, brief case, travelling bag
G/E	pausa (rises)	recess, pause
E	pausim	to make a bundle
E	pawa	power, energy, electricty
E	pe	payment, wages, reward
L	pekato (sin)	sin, trespass, transgress
?/On	pekpek	excrement, feces, manure, dung; to excrete, move one's bowels
E	peman	redeemer, paymaster
E	pen	pen, writing pen
E	pen	pain, suffering; to pain, to hurt
E	pen	paint, dye, colouring
E	penda (hinsis)	hinge
E	penda	fender, bumper, mud-guard
E	penim	to paint, dye, colour something

Origin (Ursprung)	Neo-Melanesian	English
E	pensil	pencil
Gr/E	Pentekos	Pentecost
E/L	pepa	pepper, spices, black pepper
E	pepa	paper; document, legal contract
E	pes	face, front, forehead; page; insolent, stubborn, angry
E	pesim	to contradict, be stubborn to
E	pik	pig, pork
E	pikim	to pick something, pick up
Port	pikinini	child, baby, children; any offspring, son, daughter ; the offspring of animals; fruit, seed, plant of something
E	piksa	picture, portrait, sketch; photograph, passport picture; cinema, movies; dramatisation, play; parable, allegory
L/E	pikus	certain rubber tree
E	pilai	game, entertainment, fun; to play, have a game, have fun; to be sexually engaged
E	pilim	to feel, understand, to be touched; to feel
E	pilo	pillow, wooden neck support; chock, block of wood to put under something

Origin (Ursprung)	Neo-Melanesian	English
E	pin	pin, safety pin, buckle; wooden peg; pin, hinge
E	pinas	pinnace, motor boat, launch
E	pinat (kasang)	peanut
E	pinga	finger, toe
E	pinis	end, conclusion; to be finished, be over; word to form the completive aspect of verbs
E	pinisim	to finish something; to damage, ruin, destroy
E	pinistaim	to finish one's contract
E	pinsis	pincers
E	pipel	people
?	pipi	turkey
Gaz	pipia	dirt, rubbish, leavings, scraps
E	pis	fish
E	pisin	bird
E	Pisin	New Guinea Pidgin, Neo-Melanesian
E	pislain	fishline
On	pispis	urine; to urinate, to make water
?	pitpit (tiktik)	kind of wild sugar cane; used for fences and mats; young sprouts are edible

Origin (Ursprung)	Neo-Melanesian	English
E	pius	fuse for explosives; roll of coins
E	plais	pliers
E/G	plak	flag, banner
E/G	plan	plan, sketch
E	plang	plank, board, sawn timber, lumber; wooden shield in warfare; wooden
E	planim	to plant something, put in; to bury someone
E	plantesin	plantation
E	planti	much, plenty, many
G	plasta	adhesive tape, bandage
E	plaua	flower, blossom
E	plaua	flour
E	plen (hobel)	carpenter's plane
E	plenim (hobelim)	to plane something
E	ples	place, village, town; region, area, country
E	plet	plate, dish, bowl, platter
E	plis	please; to beg, entreat
E	plis	police
E	plua	floor
E	poin	jutting point of land, cape, peninsula; to point
E	poinim	to point at, show to someone

Origin (Ursprung)	Neo-Melanesian	English
E	pok	fork
E	poketnaip (naip skru)	pocket knife
E	polis	polish, shine
E	polisim	to polish something
E	pomat	potassium permanganate, a strong disinfectant
E/L	pop (papa santu)	pope
G	popaia	to go past, overstep the mark; to miss the mark, bypass, overshoot; to slip, slide
E	popi (Katolik)	Catholic
E	popo	papaya tree and its fruit, pawpaw
Mel	por	dugout canoe without outrigger
E	poret	front, front part; forward
E	poris	porridge
E	poroman	partner
E	poromanim	to become someone's partner
E/G	pos	post, short pillar or stick
E	posin	sorcery, spell, black magic
E	pos ofis	post office
E	poteto	potato
E	poto	photo, camera, photograph; to make a photo
E	potoim	to photograph someone

Origin (Ursprung)	Neo-Melanesian	English
E	praim	to fry something
E	praipan	frying pan
E	prais	price, reward, prize, goodwill gift
E	prea	prayer; to pray
E	pren	friend; intimate companion; to be intimate with
E	prenim	to get into liaison with, to be intimate with
E	presen	present, gift (it is expected to get something in return)
E	presiden	president, chairman
E	pret	fright, fear, timidity, shyness; to be afraid
E	pretim	to frighten, threaten, scare
E	prin	printing; to print
E	prinim	to print something
E	pris	priest
Gr/E	profet	prophet
E	profit	profit, interest
E	promis	promise
E	promisim	to promise something
E	propela (karapela)	propeller

Origin (Ursprung)	Neo-Melanesian	English
E/L	Protesan	Protestant
E	prut	fruit, passion fruit
E/G	puding	pudding
Gaz	pukpuk	crocodile; person with scars (of tinea)
E	pul	oar, paddle, fin, wing; pull, drawing, stroke; to row, pull, paddle a boat
E	pulap	to be full, filled with, to abound in
E	pulapim	to fill, make something full
E	pulim	to pull, drag, tow something; to row, paddle a boat; to beg, coax, entice; to seduce, abduct
E	pulimap	to be filled
E	pulimapim	to fill something
E	pundaun	to fall, fall down; to land
?/Mel	purpur	ornamental shrubs, fringes; grass or fibre skirt for women
E	pusi	cat, pussy cat, kitten
On/E	puspus	sexual intercourse, coition; to copulate, mate
On/E	puspusim	to fecundate, impregnate someone
E	putim	to put, place; to appoint, assign

R

E	rabis	poverty, indigence; poor, downtrodden, worthless, useless; to be poor
E	rabisman	poor person, beggar
E	rabismeri	poor woman, begging woman
Mel	rai	Southeast trade wind (opposite to Northwest monsoon)
E	raifel (gan)	rifle
Mel	Raikos	Rai coast between Madang and Finschhafen
E/G	rais	rice
E	rait (sut)	on the right side
E	rait	writing, handwriting; to write
E	raithan	right hand, right side
E	raitim	to write something
E	ram (wiski)	rum
E	ran	to run, rush, fly, flow
E	ranawe	to run away
E	ranim	to chase someone
E	rapim	to rub, scour, massage
E	rat	mouse, rat

Origin (Ursprung)	Neo-Melanesian	English
E	raun (raunpela)	round, circular, spherical; around, astray; to go around, circle, make a circuit; to be dizzy, giddy
E	raunim	to surround, go around, wrap around, encircle something; to surround, to round up someone; to whirl something around
E	raunwara (tais)	pond, lake, swamp
E	raunwin	whirlwind, cyclone
G	raus	to be ousted, expelled; get out!
G	rausim	to remove, chase out, get rid of, expell, oust, kick out
E	redi	ready
E	redim	to prepare something, to get something ready
E	redio (wailis)	radio, transmitter, transmission
L/E	Refomesen	Reformation
E	refresa kos	refresher course
E	rek	rake
E	rel	rail, railing
E	relisen	religion, religious education
E	ren	rain
E	renbo	rainbow
E	resa	razor, razor blade

Origin (Ursprung)	Neo-Melanesian	English
E	resaim	to shave, cut with a razor
E	resis	race, contest; to race, compete
E	ret, retpela	red
E/G	ring	ring, circle
E	ring	to crow, ring
E	rip	reef, coral
E	ripot	report; to report
E	ripotim	to report something or someone
E	rises (pausa)	recess, recess time; to have recess
E	rit	reading; to read
E	ritim	to read something
E	riva (wara)	river
On	rokrok	frog
E	rola	roller, cylinder
E	rolaim	to roll something
E	Rom	Rome, capital of Italy
E	rong	wrong, fault, injustice, offense
E	rongim	to wrong, offend someone
E	rop	rope, cord, line string; vine, fibre, root; cluster of fruit; vein, artery, nerve umbilical cord

Origin (Ursprung)	Neo-Melanesian	English
E	ropim	to put a string on, to string
E/G	ros	rust;
		to be rusty, to rust
E	rot	road, way, path
E	rotmak	road sign
G	ruksak	haversack, knapsack
E	rula (meta)	ruler
E	rum	room, space, partition, section
E	rup	roof

S

E/G	Sabat	Sabbath, Saturday
G/E	sadel	saddle
G/E	sadelim	to saddle
E	saiden	sergeant
E	saiden mesa	sergeant major
E	Saina	China, Chinese
E	Sainaman	Chinese
E	Sainataun	Chinatown
E	sais	size, measurement
E	saisim	to size, measure

Origin (Ursprung)	Neo-Melanesian	English
E	sait	side
E	saitim	to lay something on its side
E	saitlam	sidelights on ships and cars
E	sak	shark
E	saket	jacket, coat, cloth
E	sakim	to sack, bag, put in a bag; to shake up, jostle, shove back; to contradict, disobey
L/E	sakramen	sacrament
?	saksak	sago, sago palm
G	salat	stinging nettle
E	salfa	sulfa drugs, sulfur
E	salim	to send
E	salut	salute, greeting
E	salutim	to salute, greet someone
E	samap	to sew, sew up, mend
E	samapim	to sew, mend, patch something; to hem something
E	sambai	to stand by, be ready, assist; to protect, guard someone; to lie in wait for, in ambush; to witness
E	sampela	some, others
E	samtaim	sometime, now and then
E	samting	something, a thing; and the like, or anything

Origin (Ursprung)	Neo-Melanesian	English
E	san	sun, sunshine; day, daytime; dry season
E	sanap	to stand up, stand; to rise steeply
E	sanapim	to erect something
?	sanda	oil, perfume, scented hair oil
E	sandaun	sunset, West, evening
E	Sande	Sunday
E	sande	day off, day of rest
Mel	sanguma	ritual and secret murder by means of sorcery; telepathic sorcery
Mel	sangumaman	secret ritual murderer (often on hire by sorcerers)
E	sankamap	sunrise, East, morning
E	sanpepa	sandpaper
L/E	santu (holiman)	a saint; saintly, holy, blessed
L/E	santuim	to sanctify, bless something
E	sap	shaft, axle; cutting edge, point, blade; sharp, pointed
E	sapim	to sharpen something; to carve, hew; to shave off, equalize something
E	sapnil	rafter
E	sapos	suppose, if, in case

Origin (Ursprung)	Neo-Melanesian	English
E	sapta	chapter
G	sarang (kapot)	cupboard, sideboard
E	sarap	shut up, keep quiet, be silent
E	sarapim	to silence someone, make one be quiet, to squelch
E	Sarere	Saturday
?	sarip	sickle, hoop iron to cut grass
?	saripim	to cut grass with a sarap
?	satu (daisim)	to play dice
E/G	saua	sour
E	saua	shower
E	saut	south
Sp	save	knowledge, understanding; wisdom, insight; to know, understand; to know how, be able to do; to do often, habitually
Sp	saveman	a wise man, expert, educated man
E/G	savol	shovel
E/G	savolim	to shovel, scoop up something
Mal	sayor	vegetables, greens
E	sekan	handshake, peace making
E	sekan, sekanim	to shake hands, say goodbye; to make peace
E	sekbuk	cheque book, bank book
E	seken	to agree with; to second (a parl. motion)

Origin (Ursprung)	Neo-Melanesian	English
E	seket	a circuit
E	seketeri (kuskus)	secretary
E	seksek	to be bounced about, rock around; to tremble, shake, be afraid
E	sel	shell
E	sel	canvas, sail, tarpaulin; to sail, soar
E	sela	sailor
E	sem	shame, embarrassment; genitals, private parts; to be ashamed, embarrassed
E	semineri	seminary, training centre
E	sen	chain
E	senis	exchange, substitute; to change
E	senisim	to exchange, swap, barter
E	sens	coin, cent
E	sentens	sentence
E	sentri	watcher, a lookaut, sentry; to serve as a lookout
E	Septemba	September
E/Gr	Seten	Satan, devil
E	setifiket	certificate
E	sev	shave
E	seven, sevenpela	seven, 7
E	Sevende	SDA, Seventh Day Adventist

(Ursprung) Origin	Neo-Melanesian	English
E	seventi	seventy, 70
E	seventin	seventeen, 17
E	sevim	to shave
E	si	sea, waves
E	sia	chair
E	siaman	chairman
E/Sp	siga	cigar
E/Sp	sigaret	cigarette
E	sik	sickness, disease, illness; to be sick, ill
E	siki	cheeky, insolent
E	sikis, sikispela	six, 6
E	sikman	patient, sick person
E	siling	coin: shilling
E	silva	silver
E/L	simen	cement, concrete
E/L	simenim	to cement, lay cement, fasten
E	sin (pekato)	sin
E	sindaun	to sit, sit down; to live, stay
E/G	sing	to sing
E	singaut	call, cry, sound; to call, cry, demand
E	singautim	to call for, invite, demand

Origin (Ursprung)	Neo-Melanesian	English
E	singel	single, unmarried
E	singim	to sing
E	singlis	singlet, T-shirt
E	singsing	any festival implying dancing; incantation, ritual hymn; a rocking, swaying motion; to dance, sing, jump; to sway, flutter, flap, rock
E/Gr	sinot	synod, church conference
E	sios (eklesia)	church, congregation (not building); a denomination
E	siot	shirt, blouse
E	sip	ship
E	sipsip	sheep
E	sis	cheese
E	Sisa	Caesar, emperor
E	sisel	chisel
E	siselim	to chisel something
E	sisik	to be seasick
E	sisis	scissors
E	sister	nun, European nurse
E/G	sit	remnant, remainder, left overs; feces, excrement, manure
E	sit	to cheat
E/G	sithaus	latrine, WC, toilet
E	sitim	to cheat someone

Origin (Ursprung)	Neo-Melanesian	English
E	skai	sky
E	skel	scale; portion, measure, ration; to be balanced, enough
E	skelim	to scale something; to balance something; to portion out something
E	skin	skin, hide, pod, husk, rind; body, one's person; foreskin
E	skin hat	fever, heat; to be feverish, heated
E	skin nating	naked, bare
E	skinpas	envelope
E	skinwara	perspiration, sweat
E	skirap	scraper, grater, shredder; to itch; to scratch
E	skirapim	to scrape, scratch, grate something; to tease, taunt; to provoke, sexually arouse
E	skru	screw, bolt; joint
E	skrudraiva	screwdriver
E	skruim	to screw; to join, connect something; to add, lengthen, continue

Origin (Ursprung)	Neo-Melanesian	English
E	skul	school, school house; lesson, instruction, advice; to learn, go to school
E	skulim	to teach; to correct, put someone straight
E	skulboi	schoolboy, disciple, student, pupil
E	skwea	square
E	slek	to be slack, loose; to be weak, powerless; to be lax, loose in morals; to be deflated; to slacken, ease up
E	slekim	to loosen, put slack into something; to lower by rope
E	slet	slate
E	sletpensil (grifel)	slate pencil
E	slev	slave
E	slika	silk, nylon, any shiny cloth; silky, glossy
E	sling	sling, cradle
E	slingim	to put in a sling
E	slip	sleep; to sleep, be sleepy, lie down; to lie down, lie, brood; to be in horizontal position; to have marital relations; to lean
E	slipim	to lay down lengthwise, fell; to make sleep, lull to sleep

94

(Ursprung) Origin	Neo-Melanesian	English
E	slipman	a sleepy head
E	slo (isi isi)	slow
E	smel	smell, odour, fragrance; to smell
E	smelim	to smell something
E	smelsave	to recognize by its smell
E	smok	smoke, steam, mist, haze, fog; tobacco, cigar, cigarette; to smoke
E	smokim	to smoke something; to thrash, dress down, give a good scolding or hiding
E	smol, smolpela	small, little
E	smolbrata	younger brother
E	smoldokta	medical assistant
E	smolhaus	latrine
E	smolpapa	uncle, foster father
E	snek	snake, worm, maggot, leech
E	sno	snow, cloud, fog
E	so	saw
E	so	agricultural show
E	soda	solder
E	sodaim	to solder something
E	soim	to saw something

Origin (Ursprung)	Neo-Melanesian	English
E	soim	to show
E	sok (karaide)	chalk
G	soken	stocking, sock
E	sol (tewel)	soul
E	sol	salt; salty; unpleasant, unattractive
E	sol	shoulder
E	solap	swelling; to be swollen
E	solapim	to cause to swell up, to thrash someone
E	soldia	soldier
E	solim	to salt something
E	solmarasin	epsom salts
E	solwara	salt water, sea, ocean
E	somil	sawmill
E	song	song, hymn
E	sop	soap
E	sopim	to rub with soap, put in soap
E	sop smel	perfumed soap
E	sori	compassion, mercy, charity, sympathy; sorrow, mourning; contrition; to sympathize, to feel pity for; to long for; exclamation: Golly! Ah! Well!

Origin (Ursprung)	Neo-Melanesian	English
E	sos (grevi)	sauce
E	sosaiti	a society
E	sospen	saucepan, pan, pot, kettle
E	sot, sotpela	short
E	sotwin	asthma, being short of breath; to gasp for breath
E	spaida	spider
E	spais	spice
E	spaisim	to spice, season
E	spak	to be drunk
E	spana	spanner
E	spel	a spell, off duty
E	spelim	to spell something
E	speling	spelling
E	spet	spade
E	spet	spittle, saliva, expectoration; foam, froth; to spit
E	spetim	to spit upon, spit out something
E	spia	spear, arrow
E	spiaim	to spear something, shoot with an arrow
E	spik	to speak (mostly connected with other words)

Origin (Ursprung)	Neo-Melanesian	English
E	spika	speaker (i.e. parliament)
E	spinwil	spinning wheel
E/L	spirit	methylated spirit, alcohol
E/L	spirit	spirit, soul, living part of man as opposed to body
E/L	Spirit	Holy Spirit
E	spoilim	to spoil, ruin
E	spring	spring of steel
E	spun	spoon
E	spunim	to ladle, dish out with a spoon
E	sta	star, planet
E	stan	stern, back of ship
E	standet	standard, class
E	stap	to stop, stay, remain, be; to exist, live, be present; expression for durative or continued action (whenever an English verb ends with "ing")
E	stapim	to stop someone
E	stat	start, beginning; to start
E	statim	to start something
E	stesin	station, mission station, government post, farm
E	stia	steering wheel, tiller, rudder, helm, bridle, rein; to steer, drive
E	stiabot	starboard side of a ship

Origin (Ursprung)	Neo-Melanesian	English
E	stiaim	to steer, to drive something
E	stiaman	steersman
E	stik	stick, staff, rod, cane; roll of coins
E	stil	stealing, theft, robbery; to steal; secretly, stealthily
E	stilim	to steal, take away
E	stilman	thief, robber
E/G	sting	rottenness, dirt, stench, decayed matter, bad smell; to stink, decay, rot, be rotten; stinky, rotten
E	ston	stone, rock
E	stori	story, parable; to tell a story
E	storiman	narrator, mythical authority setting facts in history
E	stov (aven)	stove
G	strafim	to punish someone
E	strena	strainer, sieve
E	strenim	to strain something
E	stret, stretpela	right, correct, O.K., proper; honest, just; smooth, even, flat, straight; exactly, directly
E	stretim	to straighten, put in order, fix, correct; to straighten, smooth, level

Origin (Ursprung)	Neo-Melanesian	English
E	stretpasin	justice, honesty, good behaviour, uprightness
E	string	string, cord
E	strong	strength, power, might
E	strong, strongpela	strong (ly), tight (ly); fervent (ly), loud (ly); hard, intensive; to insist on, demand
E	strongim	to strengthen; to encourage
E	strongpela	firm, hard, sound, solid
E	stua	store, warehouse, shop
E	stuaim	to store something
E	stuakipa	store keeper, seller
E	studen	student, pupil
E	su	shoe
E	sua	sore, wound, ulcer, abscess
E	sua	shore, beach
E	subim	to push, shove something
E	suga	sugar
Mel	sumatin	school-age child
G/E	sup	soup
G/E	supka (wilka)	wheelbarrow
?	supsup	many-pronged spear or arrow
G	surik	to move back, withdraw

| --- | --- | --- |
G	surikim	to move, pull back something
E	susa	sibling of opposite sex: for boys it is a girl, for girls it is a boy; any friend of the other sex and about the same age
E	susap	jew's-harp
Mel	susu	breast, udder; milk
Mel	susubanis	brassiere
E	sut	shot, injection; to shoot; to steer towards, set a course; to feel a stabbing pain
E	sut (rait)	right hand
?	sut	strut, brace, bracket
E	sutboi	native hunter
E	sutim	to shoot something; to inject something; to prod, hurt, poke, hit; to stab, beat; to serve, dish out; to copulate
E	sutlam (tos)	torch, flashlight
E	swim	to swim, float

Origin (Ursprung)	Neo-Melanesian	English
E	swimim	to float something; to dive for, search for
E	swis	switch
E	swisim	to switch, switch on
E	swit (switpela)	sweet, tasty, delicious; attractive, agreeable

T

G/E	tabak	tobacco (not in leaf form)
E	tablet	tablet, pill
E	taia	tyre, tire
E	taim	time; time, hour; weather, season; time of service; when, as long as, while; then, at that time
E	taims	times, multiplying
E	taipraita	typewriter
E	taipraitim	to type something
G	tais (raunwara)	pond, swamp
E	tait (haiwara)	flood tide, current
E	tait, taitpela	tight, stiff, taut
E	taitim	to tighten, stretch, pull, pull something tight

Origin (Ursprung)	Neo-Melanesian	English
E	takis	tax, customs charges
Pol	talatala	Protestant
Mel	taleo	northwest monsoon
Gaz	tambaran	ancestral spirits and ancestor worship (only men participate)
Gaz	tambaranman	one who has connection to the world of the ancestors
Gaz	tambu	small shell, used as money
Gaz	tambu	taboo; to forbid, not allow something; to sanctify, single out; to abstain, keep from; brother- or sister-in-law
Gaz	tambuim	to forbid something
E	tamiok	axe
E	tan	done, cooked
E	tang	tongue
E	tang	tank, cistern
Mel	tanget	victory leaf, shrub whose leaves are used as: sign of peace; proposal of marriage; an invitation; wrapping for sorcery; covering for buttocks

Origin (Ursprung)	Neo-Melanesian	English
E	tanim	to turn, roll, stir something; to interpret; to turn into, to become; to change one's mind, convert
E	tanimtok	interpreter
E	tantanim	to turn around, revolve, roll
E	tapiok (maniok)	starch of maniok root, an edible tuber, cassava
Gaz	taragau	hawk, eagle
?	tarangu	miserable, poor, unfortunate; to be banished, in exile; too bad! unfortunately
Pol	taro	bulbous plant, a tuber
E	tasol	only, alone, just; but, however
E	taua	tower, steeple
E	taul	towel
NI	taunam (klambu)	mosquito net
Mel	taur	Trition's trumpet shell
E	tausen	a thousand, 1,000
E	tebol	table
E	tekewe	to take away, remove, subtract, erase; to relieve, forgive
E	tekeweim	to take something away
E	tekimautim	to take something out, to harvest

Origin (Ursprung)	Neo-Melanesian	English
E	tel	tail; the thinner end of something
E	telimautim	to tell, express, reveal, make public, divulge something; to explain; to confess
E	telipon	telephone
E/L	tempel	temple
E	ten, tenpela	ten, 10
E	tenkyu	thank you; to thank someone
E	tep	tape, recording tape
E	teprikoda	tape recorder
E	teritori	territory
E	tes	test
E	testamen	testament (of Bible)
E	teti	thirty, 30
E	tetln	thirteen, 13
E	tewel	spirit, ghost, soul; reflection, image; shadow
E	ti	tea
E	tiket	ticket
?	tiktik (pitpit)	kind of wild sugar cane which is stronger than pitpit

| --- | --- | --- |
E	tilim	to deal out, divide
E	tin	tin, can
E	ting, tingting	thought, mind, memory; idea, intellect; opinion, view; to think
E	tingim	to think of, keep in mind, to consider; to remember
E	tisa	teacher
E	tisim (lainim)	to teach someone
E	tit	tooth, teeth
E	tok	word, speech, talk, message; to talk, say, speak
E	tokaut (ripot)	to tell, report, speak of something
E	tokbek	answer
E	tok bilas	mockery, ridicule
E	tok bilong bipo	fable, myth, stories of old
E	tok bokis	parable, allegory
E	tok giaman	a lie
E	tok gris	flattery, seduction
E	tok hait	mystery, secret
E	tok i go pas	foreword, introduction
E	tokim	to tell someone something
E	tok insait	conscience
E	tok kros	scolding, harsh words

Origin (Ursprung)	Neo-Melanesian	English
E	tok nogut	bad language
E	tok pilai	joke
E	tok ples	mother tongue, dialect
E	tok profet	prophecy, interpretation
E	toksave	to talk in order to make something clear
E	tok tanget	promise
E	toktok	talk, language, speech; chatter, gossip; to talk, speak, converse
E	tok tru	truth
E	tok tru antap	oath
E	tok win	rumour, idle tale
E/Sp	tomato	tomato
?	ton	tree with edible fruits
E	tos (sutlam)	electric torch, flashlight
E	trabel	difficulty, trouble; sin, fault, wrongdoing, usually with respect to sex
E	trabelim	to molest, trouble someone
E	trabelman	troublesome person, sinner
E	trabelmeri	promiscuous woman
E	traim	trial, temptation; to try, practise, test, taste

Origin (Ursprung)	Neo-Melanesian	English
E	trak	truck
E	trakta	tractor
E	trampet	trumpet, horn
E	trap	trap, rat trap
?	trausel	turtle, tortoise
E	trausis	trousers, shorts, pants
E	traut	to throw up, vomit
E	trautim	to vomit something
E	trening	training, instruction, school
E	tresara	treasurer
E	tresari	treasury
E	tret	thread
E	tretstua	trade store
E	tri (diwai)	tree
E	tri, tripela	three, 3
E	trikim	to trick someone
E	Trinde	Wednesday
L/E	Triniti	Trinity Sunday
E	Triwan	triune, three in one
E	tromoi	to throw away, let go, spend
E	tromoim	to throw something away
E	Tru	Amen

Origin (Ursprung)	Neo-Melanesian	English
E	tru, trupela	true, genuine, real; really, truly, firmly, actually; very; to be faithful, to be true
E	tu, tupela	two, 2
E	tu	too, also
E	tudak	darkness, night; dark, shady, frown
E	tude	today
E	tuhap	in two halves, parts
E	tuhat	heat, perspiration, sweat, dew; to be overheated, to sweat
E	tul	tool
E	tulait	brightness, daybreak, dawn; to be bright, shiny, coloured
E	tulip	tree with paired edible leaves
Gaz	tultul	messenger and interpreter of a chief, second in command in a village
E	tumas	too much, too many, very, very much
Gaz	tumbuan	special ancestral figures, wooden dancing masks
Gaz	tumbuna	grandfather, predecessors, ancestors; posterity from grandchildren on down
E	tumora	tomorrow
E	Tunde	Tuesday

Origin (Ursprung)	Neo-Melanesian	English
E	tupela	two, 2; along with, and
E	tupis	a pair, two pieces
Mal	tuptup	cover, lid, cork
E	twelv, twelpela	twelve, 12

U-V

Origin (Ursprung)	Neo-Melanesian	English
Gaz	umben	net for fishing or hunting
E	vaispresiden	vice-president
E	veranda	veranda, porch
E	ves	verse
E	viles (ples)	village
E	viniga (esik)	vinegar
Gaz	virua	murder, homicide
E	visita	visitor
E	vot	vote in elections
E	vot, votim	to vote for, to elect

W

E	waia	wire, cable; spear with wire prongs
E	wailis (redio)	radio, wireless set, transmission; messenger, bearer of secrets; slander, gossip
E	wailisim	to transmit, send messages
E/G	wain	wine
E	waitlewa	lung
E	wait, waitpela	white
E	waitman	white person, European
E	waitpela blut	pus
?	waitpus	paramount chief
E	waitskin	white person, European; albino
E	wan	one
E	wanai (matakiau)	one-eyed person
E	wanblut	blood relative
E	wande	once, one fine day
E	wande wande	daily, every day; now and then
E	wanem (long wanem) (na wanem) (olsem wanem)	what, which; why, for what reason; of course; how, in what way
E	wanhaus	all who live in one house
E	wankain	the same, of the same kind
E	wanlain	of the same class, clan, group; of the same origin

Origin (Ursprung)	Neo-Melanesian	English
E	wan nem	of the same name
E	wanmak	of the same size or appearance
E	wanpela	one, just one; alone, only; any; a, an (indefinite article)
E	wanpela wanpela, wan wan	one by one; each one;
E	wanpes	of the same appearance
E	wanpis	orphan, lonesome, alone
E	wanpisin	of the same tribe
E	wanples	of the same village
E	wanrot	fellow traveller; one who suffered the same experience
E	wantaim	together with, with, and; expression of similarity; expression of equality
E	wantok	same nationality, compatriot, same language group; friend, neighbour
E	wan tu	at once, immediately
E	wanwok	fellow worker
E	wara	water; watery
E	wara (riva)	river
E	wara (melek)	semen
E	wara tait (haiwara)	tide, flood, high tide

Origin (Ursprung)	Neo-Melanesian	English
E	wari	to worry
E	was (hanwas)	watch, wrist watch
E	was	to watch, guard
E	wasim	to wash something, make wet; to baptize someone
E	wasket	chin, lower jaw
E	wasmama	foster mother
E	wasman	watchman, guard, sentry; herdsman
E	waspapa	foster father, guardian
E	waswas	cleaning, bath, washing; to wash oneself, bathe; to purify oneself ritually
E	waswas (baptais)	baptism (not often used)
E	watpo	what for, why
E	we	where, where from, where to
E	wel	oil, lubricant; slipperiness; to be slippery; oily; to be sly, tricky
E	weldok	wild dog
E	welim	to oil, lubricate, anoint
E	welman	a sly, tricky person, a slick operator wild person who lives away from the village
E	wes	west
E	wesan	sand, finely grained gravel

Origin (Ursprung)	Neo-Melanesian	English
E	wet	to be wet, damp
E	wet	to wait, hesitate
E	wetim	to make something wet
E	wetim	to wait, expect, await; to hope
E	wetkot	one who is awaiting trial
E	wik	wick for lamps
E	wik	week
E	wil	wheel
E	wilbera	wheelbarrow
E	wilka (supka)	wheelbarrow
E	wilwil (baik) wilwil	bicycle; coffee mill, grinder
E	wilwilim	to grind, crush something; to turn around and around
E	win	victory; to win, excel, surpass, beat
E	win	wind, breath, air
E	win	soul, spirit
E	windo	window
E	wing	wing
E	winim	to blow on, breathe on
E	winim	to surpass someone, win over someone; to complete, finish

114

Origin (Ursprung)	Neo-Melanesian	English
E	winis	winch
E	winisim	to raise something with a winch
E	winsot (sotwin)	asthma, shortness of breath; to be short of breath
E	wip	whip
E	wipim	to whip someone
E	wisil	whistle; to whistle
E	wiskas	whiskers
E	wiski (ram)	whisky, rum, brandy etc.
E	woa	war
E	wok	work, job, task, occupation; garden, work in the gardens; to work, to be busy
E	wokabaut	walk, course, way of life; to walk, to walk around
E	wokboi	labourer, workman, employee
E	wokim	to make, build something
E	wokman	employee
E	wokmeri	working girl, housemaid
E	wul	wool

Y

Origin (Ursprung)	Neo-Melanesian	English
E	yam	yam, certain tuber (edible)
?	yambo	guava tree and its fruit
E	yang, yangpela	young, fresh
?	yar	casuarina tree
?	yau	point, ear, end (of a bag)
E	yelo, yelopela	yellow
E	yes, yesa	'yes' to positive question; 'no' to negative question
E	yes	to assent, agree
E	yesa	yes, sir; to answer someone
E	yet	still, yet; self
E	yia	year
E	yis	yeast
G	yot (aidin)	iodine
E	yu	you (singular)
E	yumi	we (including the person spoken to), us
E	yumi tupela	we two (including the person spoken to)
E	yupela	you (plural)
E	Yurop	Europe
E	yusim	to use, make use of something
E	yutupela	you two

Pilipino titles of interest from Hippocrene:

PILIPINO-ENGLISH/ENGLISH PILIPINO DICTIONARY AND PHRASEBOOK
120 pages • 3 ¾ x 7 • 0-7818-0451-5 • W • $11.95pb • (295)

PILIPINO-ENGLISH/ENGLISH-PILIPINO CONCISE DICTIONARY
389 pages • 4 x 6 • 5,000 entries • 0-87052-491-7 • W • $8.95pb • (393)

TAGALOG-ENGLISH/ENGLISH-TAGALOG (PILIPINO) DICTIONARY
500 pages • 5 x 8 • 10,000 entries • 0-7818-0683-6 • NA • $29.95hc • (745)

TAGALOG-ENGLISH/ENGLISH-TAGALOG STANDARD DICTIONARY
300 pages • 6 x 9 • 20,600 entries • 0-7818-0657-7 • W • $14.95 • (714)

Other titles of Interest:

Dictionaries

CAMBODIAN-ENGLISH/ENGLISH-CAMBODIAN STANDARD DICTIONARY
355 pp • 5 ½ x 8 ¼ • 15,000 entries • 0-87052-818-1 • NA • $8.95pb • (451)

CHINESE HANDY DICTIONARY
120 pp • 5 x 7 ¾ • 0-87052-050-4 • USA • $8.95pb • (347)

CLASSIFIED AND ILLUSTRATED CHINESE-ENGLISH DICTIONARY, REVISED
897 pp • 5 ¼ x 7 ½ • 35,000 entries • 2,000 illust • 0-87052-714-2 • NA • $19.95hc • (27)

ENGLISH-PINYIN DICTIONARY
500 pp • 4 x 6 • 10,000 entries • 0-7818-0427-2 • $19.95pb • USA • (509)

JAPANESE-ENGLISH/ENGLISH-JAPANESE CONCISE DICTIONARY, ROMANIZED
235 pp • 4 x 6 • 8,000 entries • 0-7818-0162-1 • W • $11.95pb • (474)

JAPANESE HANDY DICTIONARY
120 pp • 5 x 7 ¾ • 0-87052-962-5 • $8.95pb • NA • (466)

KOREAN-ENGLISH/ENGLISH-KOREAN PRACTICAL DICTIONARY
365 pp • 4 x 7¼ • 8,500 entries • 0-87052-092-X • Asia and NA • $14.95pb • (399)

KOREAN HANDY DICTIONARY
186 pp • 5 x 7 ¾ • 0-7818-0082-X • W • $8.95pb • (438)

THAI HANDY DICTIONARY
120 pp • 5 x 7 ¾ • 0-87052-963-3 • USA • $8.95pb • (468)

VIETNAMESE-ENGLISH/ENGLISH-VIETNAMESE STANDARD DICTIONARY
501 pp • 5 ½ x 7½ • 12,000 entries • 0-87052-924-2 • W • $19.95pb • (529)

Tutorial

CANTONESE BASIC COURSE
416 pp • 5 ½ x 8 ½ • 0-7818-0289-X • W • $19.95pb • (117)

BEGINNER'S CHINESE
150 pp • 5 ½ x 8 • 0-7818-0566-X • $14.95pb • W • (690)

MASTERING JAPANESE
368 pp • 5 ½ x 8 ½ • 0-87052-923-4 • USA • $14.95pb • (523)
2 Cassettes: • 0-87052-983-8 • USA • $12.95 • (524)

BEGINNER'S JAPANESE
200 pp • 5 ½ x 8 ½ • 0-7818-0234-2 • W • $11.95pb • (53)

LAO BASIC COURSE
350 pp • 5 ½ x 8¼ • 0-7818-0410-8 • W • $19.95pb • (470)

BEGINNER'S VIETNAMESE
517 pp • 7 x 10 • 30 lessons • 0-7818-0411-6 • $19.95pb • W • (253)

Cookbooks

THE JOY OF CHINESE COOKING
Doreen Yen Hung Feng

Includes over two hundred kitchen-tested recipes, detailed illustr‐ and a thorough index.
226 pp • 5 ½ x 7 ½ • 0-7818-0097-8 • $8.95pb • (288)

KOREA: THE FIRST WAR WE LOST, REVISED EDITION
Bevin Alexander

This bestselling account of the Korean War has now been updated with two additional chapters.

"Well researched and readable." —*The New York Times*

"This is arguably the most reliable and fully-realized one volume history of the Korean War since David Rees' *Korea.*" —*Publisher's Weekly*

"Bevin Alexander does a superb job . . .this respectable and fast-moving study is the first to be written by a professional army historian." —*Library Journal*

Bevin Alexander is a noted journalist who was a combat historian during the Korean War, commander of the 5th Historical Detachment and author of numerous battle studies for the U.S. Army. He resides in Bremo Bluff, Virginia.
580 pp • 13 maps, index • 6 x 9 • 0-7818-0577-5 • W • $19.95pb

DICTIONARY & PHRASEBOOK SERIES

AUSTRALIAN DICTIONARY AND PHRASEBOOK
131 pp • 4 3 ¾ x 7 • 1,500 entries • 0-7818-0539-2 • W • $11.95pb • (626)

BASQUE-ENGLISH/ENGLISH-BASQUE DICTIONARY AND PHRASEBOOK
240 pages • 3 ¾ x 7 • 1,500 entries • 0-7818-0622-4 • W • $11.95pb • (751)

BOSNIAN-ENGLISH/ENGLISH-BOSNIAN DICTIONARY AND PHRASEBOOK
175 pp • 3 ¾ x 7 • 1,500 entries • 0-7818-0596-1 • W • $11.95pb • (691)

BRETON-ENGLISH/ENGLISH-BRETON DICTIONARY AND PHRASEBOOK
131 pp • 3 ¾ x 7 • 1,500 entries • 0-7818-0540-6 • W • $11.95pb • (627)

BRITISH-AMERICAN/AMERICAN-BRITISH DICTIONARY AND PHRASEBOOK
160 pp • 3 ¾ x 7 • 1,400 entries • 0-7818-0450-7 • W • $11.95pb • (247)

CHECHEN-ENGLISH/ENGLISH-CHECHEN DICTIONARY AND PHRASEBOOK
160 pp • 3 ¾ x 7 • 1,400 entries • 0-7818-0446-9 • NA • $11.95pb • (183)

GEORGIAN-ENGLISH/ENGLISH-GEORGIAN DICTIONARY AND PHRASEBOOK
150 pp • 3 ¾ x 7 • 1,300 entries • 0-7818-0542-2 • W • $11.95pb • (630)

GREEK-ENGLISH/ENGLISH-GREEK DICTIONARY AND PHRASEBOOK
175 pp • 3 ¾ x 7 • 1,500 entries • 0-7818-0635-6 • W • $11.95pb • (715)

ILOCANO-ENGLISH/ENGLSIH-ILOCANO DICTIONARY AND PHRASEBOOK
266 pp • 5 12/ X 8 ½ • 0-7818-0642-9 • $14.95 •

IRISH-ENGLISH/ENGLISH-IRISH DICTIONARY AND PHRASEBOOK
160 pp • 3 ¾ x 7 • 1,400 entries/phrases • 0-87052-110-1 NA • $7.95pb • (385)

LINGALA-ENGLISH/ENGLISH-LINGALA DICTIONARY AND PHRASEBOOK
120 pp • 3 ¾ x 7 • 0-7818-0456-6 • W • $11.95pb • (296)

MALTESE-ENGLISH/ENGLISH-MALTESE DICTIONARY AND PHRASEBOOK
175 pp 3 ¾ x 7 • 1,500 entries • 0-7818-0565-1 • W • $11.95pb • (697)

POLISH DICTIONARY AND PHRASEBOOK
252 pp • 5 ½ x 8 ½ • 0-7818-0134-6 • W • $11.95pb • (192)
Cassettes—Vol I: 0-7818-0340-3 • W • $12.95 • (492)
Vol II: 0-7818-0384-5 • W • $12.95 • (486)

RUSSIAN DICTIONARY AND PHRASEBOOK, REVISED
256pp • 5 ½ x 8 ½ • 3,000 entries • 0-7818-0190-7 • W • $9.95pb • (597)

UKRAINIAN DICTIONARY AND PHRASEBOOK
205pp • 5 ½ x 8 ½ • 3,000 entries • 0-7818-0188-5 • W • $11.95pb • (28)

All prices are subject to change. To order Hippocrene Books, contact your local bookstore, call (718) 454-2366, or write to: Hippocrene Books, 171 Madison Ave. New York, NY 10016. Please enclose check or money order adding $5.00 shipping (UPS) for the first book and $.50 for each additional title.